ACADEMIA NOTES

Canadian Citizenship Test Study Guide 2025–2026 Edition

Complete Prep Based on Discover Canada: Quick Summaries, Key Facts, and 75 Practice Questions

Academia
NOTES

First published by Academia Notes a division of Madole Labs 2025

First edition

ISBN: 978-1-0691278-8-4

Contents

I

Introduction and Foundations of Canadian Citizenship

1

The Test and Preparation Strategies

1.1 About the Test

The Canadian Citizenship Test is designed to confirm that you understand Canada's history, geography, political system, values, and the rights and responsibilities of citizenship.

- **Format**: The test may be taken online or in person as part of a written or oral interview.
- **Duration**: 30 minutes.
- **Number of Questions**: 20 multiple-choice and true/false questions.
- **Passing Score**: You must answer at least 15 out of 20 questions correctly (75%).
- **Content Source**: All questions are based on Discover Canada: The Rights and Responsibilities of Citizenship (the official study guide).

> ***Pro Tip**: The test may include questions about historical dates, important people, Canadian geography, and current political leaders. Be prepared to memorize details—not just general themes.*

The basis of your preparation should be the official government publication: **Discover Canada: The Rights and Responsibilities of Citizenship**.

1.2 Required Documents and Procedures

Before the Test

Once your application is processed, you will receive an invitation letter or email with your test date, time, and location (or login instructions for an online test).

What to Bring

You must bring the following to your test appointment:

- Your test invitation letter
- Two pieces of government-issued identification (one must include a photo)
- All original documents you submitted with your citizenship application (e.g., passport, PR card, immigration records)

After the Test

- If you pass, you may be scheduled for a citizenship ceremony, where you will take the Oath of Citizenship.
- If you do not pass, you may be given a chance to retake the test. If you fail the test a second time, you will likely have an oral interview with a citizenship officer.
- In some cases, there may be a review period after you pass, while background checks and final requirements are completed before your ceremony date.

1.3 Study Methodology

The official study resource is *Discover Canada: The Rights and Responsibilities of Citizenship*. This guide is available **free** online, in print, or as an audio book.

Here are the best strategies to prepare:

Step 1: Read for the Big Picture

Do a full read-through of *Discover Canada*. Don't worry about memorization yet—get familiar with the material.

Step 2: Focus on Key Facts

Highlight or note important:

- **Dates** (e.g., Confederation: July 1, 1867)
- **Historical Figures** (e.g., Sir John A. Macdonald, Terry Fox)
- **Places** (e.g., provinces, territories, capitals, major landmarks)
- **Symbols and Values** (e.g., the maple leaf, Canadian Charter of Rights and Freedoms)

Step 3: Practice with Mock Tests

Take as many practice exams as you can. This will:

- Show you what the real test feels like
- Identify weak areas to focus on
- Improve your speed and confidence

Step 4: Use Flashcards

Make flashcards for essential facts and test yourself regularly. Flashcards are handy for memorizing:

- Prime Ministers and other leaders
- Provincial/territorial capitals
- Key historical events and dates

Step 5: Teach or Discuss

Explaining facts to a friend or family member helps lock the information into your memory.

Step 6: Review Regularly

Short, daily study sessions are more effective than cramming the night before the test.

> **Pro Tip:** *Many successful applicants report that mock tests + flashcards are the fastest way to build confidence and recall key information under time pressure.*

2

Rights, Responsibilities, and Justice

2.1 The Canadian Legal Heritage and Foundational Documents

Canada's system of government and law is built on a rich legal heritage. This heritage includes the **rule of law, freedom under the law, democratic principles, and due process**.

The Constitution and the Rule of Law

The Constitution is based on the principles that recognize the supremacy of God and the rule of law.

Rule of Law: No individual or group is above the law—not judges, politicians, or the police. Both governments and citizens must act within the law.

Sources of Law: Canadian law comes from:

- Laws passed by Parliament and provincial legislatures
- English common law traditions
- The civil code of France (applied in Quebec)
- The unwritten constitution inherited from Great Britain

Key Documents Protecting Rights

1. **Magna Carta (The Great Charter of Freedoms, 1215):** Established the principle of ordered liberty and influenced Canada's democratic tradition.
2. **The Canadian Charter of Rights and Freedoms (1982):** Added to the Constitution by Queen Elizabeth II, the Charter legally protects basic rights and freedoms for Canadians.

Pro Tip: *On the test, you may be asked about the* ***Magna Carta (1215)*** *or the* ***Charter of Rights and Freedoms (1982)****—make sure you know the dates.*

2.2 Canadian Rights and Freedoms

Fundamental Freedoms

The Charter guarantees every Canadian the following:

- Freedom of conscience and religion
- Freedom of thought, belief, opinion, and expression (including speech and the press)
- Freedom of peaceful assembly
- Freedom of association

Key Rights Under the Charter

- **Mobility Rights:** Live and work anywhere in Canada, enter and leave the country freely, and apply for a Canadian passport.
- **Official Language Rights:** French and English have equal status in Parliament and federal institutions.
- **Aboriginal Peoples' Rights:** The Charter recognizes treaty rights and does not limit or infringe upon the other rights of Indigenous peoples.

Equality and Justice

- **Equality of Women and Men:** Men and women are equal under the law. For example, a woman immigrant has the same employment opportunities as a man.
- **Habeas Corpus:** From English common law, this guarantees the right to challenge unlawful detention by the state.

Pro Tip: *The* ***four fundamental freedoms*** *and* ***mobility rights*** *are among the most commonly tested topics.*

2.3 Citizenship Responsibilities

Rights come with responsibilities. Being a citizen means contributing to Canada's democracy and community.

- **Obey the Law:** Everyone must follow Canada's laws.
- **Take Responsibility for Oneself and Family:** Supporting yourself and your family contributes to dignity and prosperity.
- **Serve on a Jury:** Jury duty is a legal obligation and a privilege reserved for Canadian citizens.
- **Vote in Elections:** At all levels—federal, provincial/territorial, and municipal.
- **Help Others in the Community:** Volunteering builds stronger, more caring communities.
- **Protect Canada's Heritage and Environment:** Safeguarding cultural traditions and natural resources ensures they endure for future generations

☞ *Note:* Learning both official languages is strongly encouraged, but it is **not a legal requirement** for citizenship.

2.4 The Justice System

Canada's justice system ensures fairness and protects rights through an organized framework of laws.

Core Legal Principles

- **Presumption of Innocence:** Every person is considered innocent until proven guilty.
- **Due Process:** The government must respect all the legal rights guaranteed under the law.

The Three Branches of Government

The justice system is part of Canada's democratic structure:

1. **Executive:** Prime Minister and Cabinet
2. **Legislative:** Parliament (Sovereign, Senate, House of Commons)
3. **Judicial:** Courts

The Courts

- **Supreme Court of Canada:** The highest court; decisions are final. There are nine judges, appointed by the Governor General.
- **Federal Court of Canada:** Deals with matters such as immigration, patents, and federal disputes.
- **Trial Courts (e.g., Court of Queen's Bench):** Handle serious criminal and civil cases at the provincial level.
- **Small Claims Courts:** Provincial courts that handle minor civil disputes.

Policing and Legal Aid

The role of the police is to maintain public safety and enforce the law.

Police Forces:

The **Royal Canadian Mounted Police (RCMP)** is Canada's national police force. It enforces federal laws and acts as the provincial police in every province and territory **except Ontario and Quebec**. Ontario and Quebec have their own provincial police forces. Some municipalities operate their own local police services.

- **Public Accountability:** Canadians have the right to question the conduct of police officers.
- **Legal Aid:** If you cannot afford a lawyer, legal aid services are available at low or no cost in most communities.

> ***Pro Tip:*** *Expect test questions on the* ***Supreme Court of Canada****, the* ***role of the RCMP****, and the principle of* ***presumption of innocence****.*

2.5 Chapter 2 Review Questions

Test your knowledge of rights, responsibilities, and justice in Canada.

Questions

Which historic document first established the principle that no person, not even the king, is above the law?

a) The Canadian Charter of Rights and Freedoms
b) The Constitution Act, 1867
c) The Magna Carta
d) The Bill of Rights (1960)

Which of the following is ***not*** *one of the four fundamental freedoms* *guaranteed by the Charter?*

a) Freedom of conscience and religion

b) Freedom of thought, belief, opinion, and expression

c) Freedom of property ownership

d) Freedom of peaceful assembly

What are ***mobility rights*** *under the Charter?*

a) The right to free healthcare anywhere in Canada

b) The right to live and work anywhere in Canada, enter/leave freely, and apply for a passport

c) The right to own property in any province

d) The right to drive in every province without a license

Who serves as Canada's national police force and also provides provincial policing in every province except Ontario and Quebec?

a) Provincial Police Service

b) The Royal Canadian Mounted Police (RCMP)

c) The Supreme Court of Canada

d) Municipal Police

What principle of Canadian law means everyone is considered innocent until proven guilty?

a) Rule of Law

b) Habeas Corpus

c) Presumption of Innocence

d) Due Process

* * *

Answer Key

1. c) The Magna Carta
2. c) Freedom of property ownership
3. b) The right to live and work anywhere in Canada, enter/leave freely, and apply for a passport
4. b) The Royal Canadian Mounted Police (RCMP)
5. c) Presumption of Innocence

II

The Land, The People, and National Identity

3

Geography and Regions

3.1 Canadian Geography and Regions

Canada is the **second-largest country in the world**, covering nearly 10 million square kilometres.

Continental Structure and Borders

Oceans: Canada is bordered by three oceans:

- Pacific Ocean (west)
- Atlantic Ocean (east)
- Arctic Ocean (north)

Border with the United States: Canada shares the **longest undefended border in the world** with the U.S. Millions of people cross safely every year.

Capital: Ottawa is Canada's national capital, chosen by **Queen Victoria in 1857**.

Political Divisions and Demographics

- **Provinces and Territories:** 10 provinces + 3 territories = 13 political divisions.
- **Population:** Over **34 million people** (Discover Canada's reference point, though the current population exceeds 40 million).
- **Centralization:** More than half live in Southern Quebec and Ontario, near the Great Lakes and St. Lawrence River.
- **Largest Province by Population:** Ontario (over one-third of Canadians).
- **The Great Lakes:** Ontario borders four of them (Superior, Huron, Erie, and Ontario), with **Lake Michigan** entirely in the U.S.

The Five Regions of Canada

1. The Atlantic Provinces

- **Newfoundland and Labrador:** Most easterly point in North America; own time zone; joined Confederation in **1949**.
- **Prince Edward Island (PEI):** Smallest province; connected by the **Confederation Bridge**.
- **Nova Scotia:** Most populous Atlantic province; capital Halifax has Canada's largest naval base. Historically strong in coal, forestry, and farming.
- **New Brunswick:** The **only officially bilingual province**.

2. Central Canada

- **Ontario & Quebec:** The industrial and manufacturing heartland. Together, they produce over three-quarters of Canadian-manufactured goods.
- **Toronto:** The largest city and main financial hub.
- **Quebec:** Largest producer of hydroelectricity; leader in pulp and paper.

3. The Prairie Provinces

- **Manitoba, Saskatchewan, Alberta:** Known for agriculture and energy.
- **Saskatchewan:** "Wheat province," leading producer of grains and oilseeds (40% of Canada's arable land).
- **Alberta:** Largest producer of oil and gas.

4. The West Coast

- **British Columbia (B.C.):** Canada's Pacific gateway.
- **Port of Vancouver:** Largest and busiest port, vital for trade with Asia.
- **Forestry:** Most valuable in Canada.
- **Okanagan Valley:** Famous for orchards and wineries.

5. The Northern Territories

- **Yukon, Northwest Territories, Nunavut:** Together, more than one-third of Canada's land mass.
- **"Land of the Midnight Sun":** In summer, daylight can last 24 hours.
- **Nunavut:** Created in **1999**, capital is Iqaluit.
- **Resources:** Gold, lead, zinc.
- **Yukon Gold Rush:** Attracted thousands of miners in the 1890s.

> ***Pro Tip:*** *Remember the* ***five regions of Canada and which provinces belong to each****. This is a frequent test question.*

3.2 The Founding Peoples and Diversity in Canada

Canada was built upon three founding peoples: the **Indigenous (Aboriginal)**, the **French**, and the **British**.

Aboriginal Peoples

- **First Nations:** Largest Indigenous group. Band Chiefs and Councillors govern many communities.
- **Inuit:** Means "the people" in Inuktitut; they live in small, scattered communities across the Arctic.
- **Métis:** Distinct people of mixed Aboriginal and European ancestry. Most live in the Prairie Provinces. Historically, they were traders, guides, and interpreters.

History and Rights:

- **Residential Schools:** Operated from 1800s–1980s, aimed to assimilate Indigenous children. Poorly funded and harmful, Canada formally apologized in **2008**.
- **Voting Rights:** Indigenous peoples gained the right to vote federally in **1960**.

Official Languages and Identity

- **English and French:** Both are official languages with equal status in federal institutions.
- **Anglophones:** English first-language speakers.
- **Francophones:** French first-language speakers (most in Quebec).
- **Acadians:** Descendants of French settlers in the Maritimes (since 1604).
- **Quebecers/Quebecois:** People of Quebec. In 2006, the House of Commons recognized them as a nation within a united Canada.
- **New Brunswick:** The only officially bilingual province.

Diversity and Culture

- **Multiculturalism:** Official policy since **1971**, central to Canadian identity.
- **Immigration:** Since the 1970s, most newcomers have come from Asia.

- **Religion:** Catholicism remains the largest religious affiliation.

> ***Pro Tip:*** *Key dates to know — **1960** (Indigenous voting rights), **1971** (multiculturalism policy), **2008** (residential school apology).*

3.3 Chapter 3 Review Questions

Questions

Which city was chosen by Queen Victoria in 1857 as Canada's capital?

a) Toronto
b) Ottawa
c) Montreal
d) Quebec City

Which province is the only officially bilingual province in Canada?

a) Quebec
b) Manitoba
c) New Brunswick
d) Ontario

Which province is often called the "wheat province"?

a) Manitoba
b) Saskatchewan
c) Alberta
d) Quebec

When did Nunavut officially become a territory of Canada?

a) 1867
b) 1949
c) 1982

d) 1999

When were Indigenous peoples granted the right to vote in federal elections?

a) 1867

b) 1949

c) 1960

d) 1982

* * *

Answer Key

1. b) Ottawa
2. c) New Brunswick
3. b) Saskatchewan
4. d) 1999
5. c) 1960

4

Who Canadians Are

4.1 Early Exploration and New France (Pre-1763)

The First Europeans

- Indigenous peoples were Canada's first inhabitants, arriving thousands of years ago from Asia.
- Around 1000 AD, Vikings from Iceland colonized Greenland and reached Newfoundland and Labrador.

Key Early Explorers

- **John Cabot (1497):** Italian immigrant to England who mapped Canada's East Coast and claimed "New Founde Land" for England.
- **Jacques Cartier (1534–1542):** Made three voyages for France. The word *kanata* (Iroquoian for "village") inspired the name *Canada*.

Building a French Empire

- **1604:** Pierre de Monts and Samuel de Champlain founded a settlement in Acadia (Nova Scotia).
- **1608:** Champlain built Québec City.
- **Fur Trade:** French and Indigenous peoples worked together in the fur trade. Leaders included Jean Talon, Bishop Laval, and Count Frontenac.
- **Hudson's Bay Company (1670):** Granted exclusive trading rights by King Charles II. French traders known as voyageurs and coureurs des bois travelled by canoe to trade furs.

Struggle for the Continent

- **1759:** The Battle of the Plains of Abraham (Québec City). The British defeated the French, ending France's empire in North America. Both commanders, James Wolfe (British) and Montcalm (French), were killed.

> ***Pro Tip:*** *Remember* ***1608 (Quebec City), 1670 (Hudson's Bay Company), 1759 (Plains of Abraham)****. These dates come up often.*

4.2 From Colony to Nationhood (1774–1867)

Constitutional Milestones

- **Quebec Act (1774):** Guaranteed Catholic religious freedom, restored French civil law, and kept British criminal law.
- **United Empire Loyalists (1776+):** Over 40,000 Loyalists fled the American Revolution to settle in Nova Scotia and Quebec.
- **Constitutional Act (1791):** Split Quebec into Upper Canada (English-speaking) and Lower Canada (French-speaking). Both had elected assemblies.

War, Abolition, and Responsible Government

- **War of 1812:** U.S. invasion repelled by British, Canadians and First Nations (notably Chief Tecumseh). Laura Secord became a heroine.
- **Abolition of Slavery:** In 1793, Upper Canada banned new slaves under Governor John Graves Simcoe. Canada became a destination on the Underground Railroad.
- **Responsible Government (1847–48):** Nova Scotia was the first province to adopt this system. In 1849, Sir Louis-Hippolyte La Fontaine led the first responsible government in the Canadas.

Confederation and Western Expansion

- **1867 (Dominion of Canada):** The British North America Act created Canada with four provinces: Ontario, Quebec, Nova Scotia, and New Brunswick.
- **Fathers of Confederation:** Key leaders included Sir John A. Macdonald (first Prime Minister) and Sir George-Étienne Cartier.
- **Manitoba and Louis Riel (1870):** Riel led a Métis uprising at Fort Garry, leading to the creation of Manitoba.
- **Canadian Pacific Railway (completed 1885):** Linked east and west, bringing British Columbia into Confederation in 1871. Built with both European and Chinese labour.
- **North West Mounted Police (1873):** Later became the RCMP, policing the West. Sir Sam Steele was a famous Mountie hero.

***Pro Tip:** Confederation = **1867**, CPR completed = **1885**, RCMP founded = **1873**.*

4.3 World Wars and Postwar Canada

The Great Wars

- **Women's Suffrage:** Led by Dr. Emily Stowe. Manitoba was first (1916). Federal vote for women in 1918. Agnes Macphail became the first woman

MP (1921).

- **First World War (1914–18):** 600,000 served, 60,000 died. Vimy Ridge (1917) was a defining Canadian victory under General Arthur Currie. The Peace Tower (1927) commemorates WWI.
- **Remembrance Day (Nov 11):** Canadians wear the poppy and observe a moment of silence. 110,000 Canadians have died in service to date.
- **Second World War (1939–45):** Over 1 million served. Canada trained 130,000 Allied aircrew. On D-Day (June 6, 1944), 15,000 Canadians landed at Juno Beach. Canada also liberated the Netherlands. By war's end, Canada had the world's third-largest navy.

Postwar Society and Modernization

- **1949:** Newfoundland and Labrador joined Confederation.
- **1960:** Indigenous peoples gained the right to vote federally.
- **1960s Quiet Revolution (Quebec):** Period of rapid social change.
- **Official Languages Act (1969):** Guaranteed French and English services in the federal government.
- **1982:** Constitution amended; the **Charter of Rights and Freedoms** was added, proclaimed by **Queen Elizabeth II**. Canada gained full constitutional independence.
- **1999: Nunavut** was created as a territory, with its capital at Iqaluit.

4.4 Great Canadian Achievements and Symbols

Discoveries and Inventions

- **Insulin:** Sir Frederick Banting & Charles Best.
- **Telephone:** Alexander Graham Bell.
- **Standard Time Zones:** Sir Sandford Fleming.
- **Radio:** Reginald Fessenden.
- **Snowmobile:** Joseph-Armand Bombardier.
- **BlackBerry:** Created by RIM (Mike Lazaridis & Jim Balsillie).

Canadian Heroes and Honours

- **Victoria Cross (V.C.):** Canada's highest military honour, awarded 96 times since 1854.
- **Terry Fox:** Launched the Marathon of Hope (1980) for cancer research.
- **Rick Hansen:** Completed the "Man in Motion" world tour (1985) for spinal cord research.
- **Dr. Wilder Penfield:** Famous brain surgeon at McGill.
- **Donovan Bailey:** Olympic gold sprinter, world record holder (1996).

> ***Pro Tip:*** Vimy Ridge (1917), D-Day Juno Beach (1944), and Confederation (1867) *are almost guaranteed question topics.*

4.5 Chapter 4 Review Questions

Questions

Which French explorer founded Québec City in 1608?
 a) John Cabot
 b) Samuel de Champlain
 c) Jacques Cartier
 d) Count Frontenac

What was the significance of the Quebec Act of 1774?
 a) It created the Canadian Charter of Rights and Freedoms
 b) It granted religious freedom for Catholics and restored French civil law
 c) It abolished slavery in Upper Canada
 d) It divided Quebec into Upper and Lower Canada

Which Canadian victory in 1917 is often considered a defining moment for Canada as a nation?
 a) Battle of Juno Beach
 b) Battle of Vimy Ridge

c) Battle of the Plains of Abraham
d) Liberation of the Netherlands

When did Newfoundland and Labrador join Confederation?

a) 1867
b) 1871
c) 1949
d) 1999

Who is remembered for starting the Marathon of Hope to raise money for cancer research?

a) Rick Hansen
b) Donovan Bailey
c) Terry Fox
d) Sir Sandford Fleming

* * *

Answer Key

1. b) Samuel de Champlain
2. b) It granted religious freedom for Catholics and restored French civil law
3. b) Battle of Vimy Ridge
4. c) 1949
5. c) Terry Fox

III

How Canada is Governed

5

Canada's Economy

5.1 Canada's System of Government

Canada's government rests on **three core principles**:

1. Canada is a **federal state** (power shared between federal, provincial, and municipal governments).
2. Canada is a **parliamentary democracy** (citizens elect representatives).
3. Canada is a **constitutional monarchy** (the Head of State is the Sovereign).

Foundational Principles

- **Supremacy of God and Rule of Law:** The Constitution recognizes these as guiding principles.
- **"Peace, Order, and Good Government":** A phrase from the **British North America Act (1867)** that defines Canada's governing philosophy.

Three Branches of Government:

1. **Executive** → Prime Minister and Cabinet
2. **Legislative** → Parliament (Sovereign, Senate, House of Commons)

3. **Judicial** → Courts

Head of State vs. Head of Government

- **Head of State:** The Sovereign (King or Queen).
- **Head of Government:** The Prime Minister.

> ***Pro Tip:*** *A common test trick is asking whether the PM or the King is Head of State. The correct answer:* ***The Sovereign is Head of State; the Prime Minister is Head of Government.***

5.2 The Crown and Its Representatives

The Sovereign

- A hereditary monarch who reigns in accordance with Canada's Constitution.
- Symbol of sovereignty, allegiance, and constitutional freedom.
- Citizens pledge loyalty to the Sovereign, not to a document or a flag.
- The **Royal Anthem** is *God Save the King (or Queen).*

Representatives of the Crown

1. **Governor General (federal):** Represents the Sovereign at the national level. Appointed on the advice of the Prime Minister for about 5 years. Grants **Royal Assent** to bills and performs ceremonial duties.
2. **Lieutenant Governor (provincial):** Represents the Sovereign in each province. Signs bills into law at the provincial level.
3. **Commissioner (territorial):** Represents the federal government in territories (ceremonial role, not the Sovereign).

5.3 The Legislative and Executive Branches

Parliament and Law-Making

- **Parliament:** Sovereign, Senate, and House of Commons.
- **House of Commons:** Elected Members of Parliament (MPs) represent ridings (constituencies).
- **Senate:** Senators are appointed on the advice of the PM, and serve until the age of 75.
- **Bills:** Proposed laws. To pass, a bill must be approved by both Houses and receive **Royal Assent** from the Governor General.

Prime Minister and Cabinet

- **Prime Minister:** Leader of the party with the most MPs; invited by the Governor General to form a government.
- **Cabinet:** Ministers chosen by the PM, usually MPs. They manage federal departments, prepare budgets, and propose laws.
- **Confidence of the House:** The government must retain the majority support of MPs.
- **Majority government:** Holds more than half of the seats.
- **Minority government:** Holds fewer than half; must cooperate with other parties.
- **Opposition:** Parties not in power. The largest opposition party is the **Official Opposition**.

> ***Pro Tip:*** *A test question might ask:* What happens if a government loses the confidence of the House? *Answer:* ***It must resign or call an election.***

5.4 Federalism: Division of Powers

Canada is a **federal state**, which means responsibilities are divided among different levels of government. Each level has specific powers defined in the **Constitution Act, 1867**.

Federal Government

- The federal government handles matters that affect the whole country.
- Key responsibilities include: national defence, foreign policy, international trade, currency, criminal law, and citizenship.
- The federal government is led by the Prime Minister and elected Members of Parliament (MPs).

Provincial and Territorial Governments

- Provinces and territories are responsible for areas that directly affect daily life, such as education, health care, natural resources, highways, and property and civil rights.
- Each province is led by a Premier and elected representatives (called MLAs, MNAs, MPPs, or MHAs, depending on the province or territory).

Shared Responsibilities

- Some areas are shared between federal and provincial governments, such as agriculture and immigration.

Municipal Governments

- Municipal or local governments are created by provincial and territorial legislatures.
- They manage community needs, including passing bylaws, garbage and snow removal, firefighting, public transit, and local health and social

services.

- The head of a municipal government is usually a **Mayor** or **Reeve**, supported by a council.

5.5 Elections and the Judicial System

Federal Elections

- **Timing:** Held every 4 years on the **third Monday in October**.
- **Eligibility to Vote:** Must be a Canadian citizen, at least 18, and on the voters' list.
- **Elections Canada:** Independent agency that manages federal elections. Issues voter information cards.
- **Secret Ballot:** Your vote is confidential; no one can force you to reveal it.
- **Running for Office:** Any Canadian citizen age 18+ may run.

The Judicial System

- **Rule of Law:** The law applies to everyone equally.
- **Presumption of Innocence:** Everyone is innocent until proven guilty.

Courts:

- **Supreme Court of Canada:** Highest court, 9 judges appointed by the Governor General.
- **Federal Court:** Handles national issues.
- **Trial/Small Claims Courts:** Handle civil and local disputes.

Police: Enforce laws and keep people safe. The **RCMP** serves federally and as provincial police except in Ontario and Quebec.

Juries: Only citizens may serve. Jury duty is a legal obligation.

Legal Aid: Available for people who cannot afford a lawyer.

5.6 Chapter 5 Review Questions

Questions

Which phrase from the Constitution defines Canada's governing philosophy?

a) Life, Liberty, and the Pursuit of Happiness
b) Peace, Order, and Good Government
c) Liberty, Equality, Fraternity
d) Justice for All

Who is Canada's Head of State?

a) Prime Minister
b) Governor General
c) The Sovereign (King/Queen)
d) The Senate

What is the role of the Governor General?

a) Head of Government
b) Signs bills into law and represents the Sovereign
c) Oversees provincial governments
d) Acts as the head of the Supreme Court

Which of the following is NOT a federal government responsibility?

a) National Defence
b) Education
c) International Trade
d) Citizenship

What happens if the government loses a confidence vote in the House of Commons?

a) The Supreme Court takes over temporarily
b) The Governor General resigns
c) The government must resign or call an election
d) The opposition parties are dissolved

* * *

Answer Key

1. b) Peace, Order, and Good Government
2. c) The Sovereign (King/Queen)
3. b) Signs bills into law and represents the Sovereign
4. b) Education
5. c) The government must resign or call an election

6

Symbols and National Achievements

6.1 National Symbols and Identity

Canada's symbols represent its history, traditions, and values.

- **National Flag:** First raised in **1965**, featuring the red maple leaf. The red and white colours were proclaimed national colours in **1921**.
- **Maple Leaf:** Canada's best-known symbol, used as early as the 1700s by French Canadians.
- **Beaver:** Associated with the Hudson's Bay Company; appears on the five-cent coin.
- **Coat of Arms and Motto:** Adopted after WWI. The motto is *"A mari usque ad mare"* ("From sea to sea"). The arms include symbols of England, France, Scotland, and Ireland.
- **The Crown:** Symbol of the state for more than 400 years; represents government, legislatures, courts, police, and the military.
- **Parliament Buildings:** The Peace Tower was completed in **1927** in memory of WWI.
- **Royal Anthem:** *God Save the King (or Queen).*
- **National Anthem:** *O Canada* became the official anthem in **1980**. Its last line is *"O Canada, we stand on guard for thee."*

Sports and Leisure

- **National Winter Sport:** Ice hockey, Canada's most popular spectator sport. The Stanley Cup was donated in **1892** by Lord Stanley.
- **Official Summer Sport:** Lacrosse, originally played by Indigenous peoples.
- **Other Sports:** Canadian football is the second most popular spectator sport; soccer has the most registered players. Basketball was invented by Canadian James Naismith in 1891.

6.2 Great Canadian Achievements and Honours

Discoveries and Inventions

- **Insulin:** Discovered by Sir Frederick Banting and Charles Best, it has saved millions of lives.
- **Standard Time Zones:** Created by Sir Sandford Fleming.
- **Telephone:** Invented by Alexander Graham Bell.
- **Radio:** Reginald Fessenden sent the world's first wireless voice message.
- **Snowmobile:** Invented by Joseph-Armand Bombardier.
- **BlackBerry:** Created by RIM, founded by Mike Lazaridis and Jim Balsillie.
- **Cardiac Pacemaker:** Invented by Dr. John A. Hopps.
- **Neuroscience:** Dr. Wilder Penfield was a pioneering brain surgeon, once called "the greatest living Canadian."

Heroes and Honours

- **Victoria Cross (V.C.):** Canada's highest military honour, awarded for exceptional bravery and awarded to 96 Canadians since 1854.
- **Terry Fox:** Lost his leg to cancer; began the **Marathon of Hope (1980)** to raise money for cancer research.
- **Rick Hansen:** Completed the **Man in Motion Tour (1985)**, circling the globe in a wheelchair for spinal cord research.
- **General Sir Arthur Currie:** Canada's greatest soldier in WWI.

- **Donovan Bailey:** Sprinter, double Olympic gold medalist, world record holder at the 1996 Olympics.

6.3 Public Holidays and Important Dates

- **January 1:** New Year's Day
- **January 11:** Sir John A. Macdonald Day
- **April 9:** Vimy Day (commemorates Canadian victory in 1917)
- **Victoria Day:** Monday before May 25 (Sovereign's birthday)
- **July 1:** Canada Day (Confederation, 1867)
- **First Monday in September:** Labour Day
- **Second Monday in October:** Thanksgiving Day
- **November 11:** Remembrance Day (honours veterans and fallen soldiers)
- **November 20:** Sir Wilfrid Laurier Day
- **December 25:** Christmas Day
- **December 26:** Boxing Day

> ***Pro Tip:** Be prepared for questions on **Canada Day, Remembrance Day,** and **Vimy Day**. These are often highlighted in practice tests.*

6.4 Chapter 6 Review Questions

Questions

What percentage of Canadians work in service industries?

a) 50%
b) 60%
c) 75%
d) 90%

Which province is the largest producer of hydroelectricity?

a) Alberta
b) British Columbia

c) Quebec
d) Saskatchewan

When was the National Flag of Canada first raised?
a) 1867
b) 1921
c) 1965
d) 1980

Who discovered insulin, saving millions of lives worldwide?
a) Alexander Graham Bell and Reginald Fessenden
b) Sir Frederick Banting and Charles Best
c) Joseph-Armand Bombardier and Mike Lazaridis
d) Dr. Wilder Penfield and Dr. John A. Hopps

What is celebrated on April 9 each year in Canada?
a) Canada Day
b) Sir John A. Macdonald Day
c) Vimy Day
d) Remembrance Day

* * *

Answer Key

1. c) 75%
2. c) Quebec
3. c) 1965
4. b) Sir Frederick Banting and Charles Best
5. c) Vimy Day

IV

Preparing for Citizenship

7

The Citizenship Ceremony and Next Steps

Passing the Canadian Citizenship Test is an important milestone, but it is not the final step. To officially become a Canadian citizen, you must attend a **citizenship ceremony** and take the **Oath of Citizenship**. This ceremony marks the formal moment you join the Canadian family as a full citizen.

The Citizenship Ceremony

Invitation

Once your application is approved and you have passed the test and interview, you will receive a notice to attend a citizenship ceremony. This letter or email will tell you the date, time, and location of your ceremony.

The Oath of Citizenship

At the ceremony, all applicants stand together to take the **Oath of Citizenship**. By swearing or affirming the oath, you make a solemn promise to:

- Be loyal to Canada and its Sovereign
- Obey Canada's laws
- Fulfill your duties as a citizen

The oath is taken before a citizenship judge or presiding official. After reciting the oath, you are presented with your **citizenship certificate**.

The Meaning of the Oath

Taking the Oath of Citizenship is more than a legal requirement — it is a pledge of loyalty and commitment. It unites all Canadians, no matter their background, in a shared responsibility to uphold the country's values and freedoms.

What to Expect at the Ceremony

- **Dress and Presentation:** Ceremonies are dignified and formal. Many people choose to wear business attire or traditional cultural clothing.
- **Family and Friends:** Guests are usually welcome, and it is common to celebrate with loved ones after the ceremony.
- **Receiving Your Certificate:** The **citizenship certificate** proves your new status. Keep it safe, as you will need it for important purposes such as applying for a Canadian passport.

Life as a Canadian Citizen

Becoming a citizen brings both **new rights** and **ongoing responsibilities**:

- You may now **vote** in federal, provincial, territorial, and municipal elections.
- You are eligible to **run for political office**.
- You can apply for a **Canadian passport**, one of the most respected travel documents in the world.
- You share in the duty to obey the law, serve on juries when called, and contribute to your community.

Citizenship is both a privilege and a commitment. By taking the oath, you join millions of Canadians in building a democratic, diverse, and free society.

Looking Ahead

Your journey does not end at the ceremony — it truly begins there. Whether you participate in elections, volunteer in your community, or simply live out Canadian values in your daily life, your actions help strengthen the country.

Canada thrives when its citizens are informed, active, and proud. You are now part of that story.

8

Practice Questions and Answers

1. What are the two official languages of Canada?

a) English and French

b) English and Spanish

c) French and Cree

d) English and Inuktitut

2. What is the capital city of Canada?

a) Toronto

b) Ottawa

c) Montreal

d) Vancouver

3. What year did Canada become a country?

a) 1812

b) 1867

c) 1871

d) 1885

4. Which provinces were the first four to join Confederation?

a) Ontario, Quebec, Nova Scotia, New Brunswick

b) Ontario, Quebec, Prince Edward Island, Newfoundland

c) Ontario, Quebec, Manitoba, British Columbia
d) Quebec, Nova Scotia, New Brunswick, Prince Edward Island

5. Who was Canada's first Prime Minister?
a) Sir Wilfrid Laurier
b) Sir John A. Macdonald
c) Sir George-Étienne Cartier
d) Lester B. Pearson

6. What is the meaning of the motto on Canada's Coat of Arms, *"A mari usque ad mare"*?
a) Peace, Order, and Good Government
b) From Sea to Sea
c) Truth and Justice
d) Unity in Diversity

7. Which province is the only one officially bilingual?
a) Quebec
b) Ontario
c) New Brunswick
d) Manitoba

8. Who are Canada's Indigenous peoples?
a) First Nations, Inuit, and Métis
b) Acadians, Loyalists, and Métis
c) French, British, and Loyalists
d) Algonquin, Cree, and Mohawk

9. What was the significance of the Battle of Vimy Ridge in 1917?
a) The U.S. declared war on Germany
b) It was a defining moment for Canada as a nation
c) It ended the First World War
d) It began women's right to vote

10. Who is the Head of State in Canada?

a) The Prime Minister

b) The Governor General

c) The Sovereign (King or Queen)

d) The Speaker of the House

11. Who is the Head of Government in Canada?

a) The Prime Minister

b) The Sovereign

c) The Governor General

d) The Senate

12. What do Canadians wear on Remembrance Day to honour veterans?

a) A red ribbon

b) A red maple leaf

c) A red poppy

d) A medal

13. What is the national winter sport of Canada?

a) Lacrosse

b) Hockey

c) Curling

d) Skiing

14. Which sport was invented by Canadian James Naismith in 1891?

a) Soccer

b) Basketball

c) Baseball

d) Football

15. Who discovered insulin, saving millions of lives?

a) Alexander Graham Bell and Reginald Fessenden

b) Sir Frederick Banting and Charles Best

c) Joseph-Armand Bombardier and Mike Lazaridis

d) Dr. Wilder Penfield and Dr. John A. Hopps

16. What is celebrated on July 1 each year?

a) Labour Day

b) Remembrance Day

c) Canada Day

d) Vimy Day

17. Which province joined Confederation in 1949?

a) Alberta

b) Newfoundland and Labrador

c) Prince Edward Island

d) Saskatchewan

18. What does the Crown symbolize in Canada?

a) The monarchy only

b) The government, including Parliament, legislatures, courts, police, and military

c) Freedom of speech

d) The rule of law

19. Which province is the largest by population?

a) Quebec

b) Ontario

c) Alberta

d) British Columbia

20. Which province is the largest by land area?

a) Alberta

b) Ontario

c) Quebec

d) British Columbia

21. What is the capital city of Quebec?

a) Montreal
b) Quebec City
c) Sherbrooke
d) Ottawa

22. Which ocean borders Canada to the east?

a) Pacific Ocean
b) Atlantic Ocean
c) Arctic Ocean
d) Indian Ocean

23. What was the purpose of the Quebec Act of 1774?

a) To abolish slavery
b) To guarantee religious freedom for Catholics and restore French civil law
c) To create Confederation
d) To give women the right to vote

24. Who led the Métis in defending their rights and is known as the Father of Manitoba?

a) Chief Tecumseh
b) Louis Riel
c) Sir George-Étienne Cartier
d) John Graves Simcoe

25. Who was Canada's greatest soldier in the First World War?

a) Sir Arthur Currie
b) General Montgomery
c) James Wolfe
d) Marquis de Montcalm

26. What is the role of the Governor General?

a) Head of Government

b) Represents the Sovereign and grants Royal Assent to bills
c) Oversees provincial governments
d) Leads the Supreme Court

27. What is Canada's system of government?
a) Republic
b) Federal state, parliamentary democracy, and constitutional monarchy
c) Dictatorship
d) Absolute monarchy

28. What is Canada's highest court?
a) Federal Court
b) Court of Appeal
c) Supreme Court of Canada
d) Court of Queen's Bench

29. What principle means everyone is innocent until proven guilty?
a) Rule of Law
b) Habeas Corpus
c) Presumption of Innocence
d) Due Process

30. Which act established Canada as a self-governing Dominion in 1867?
a) British North America Act
b) Constitution Act, 1982
c) Quebec Act
d) Constitutional Act

31. Which province is the main producer of oil and gas in Canada?
a) Saskatchewan
b) Ontario
c) Quebec
d) Alberta

32. Which province is the largest producer of hydroelectricity?

a) Alberta

b) Quebec

c) British Columbia

d) Manitoba

33. Which province is known as the "wheat province"?

a) Saskatchewan

b) Alberta

c) Manitoba

d) Ontario

34. Who is the Premier of a province similar to at the federal level?

a) A judge

b) The Prime Minister

c) The Governor General

d) The Speaker of the House

35. Which is Canada's largest city and financial centre?

a) Ottawa

b) Montreal

c) Toronto

d) Vancouver

36. Which Canadian province is the smallest in land area?

a) Prince Edward Island

b) Nova Scotia

c) New Brunswick

d) Newfoundland and Labrador

37. Which Canadian province has its own time zone?

a) British Columbia

b) Quebec

c) Newfoundland and Labrador
d) Manitoba

38. Who was the first French explorer to establish permanent settlements in Canada?
a) Jacques Cartier
b) Samuel de Champlain
c) Pierre de Monts
d) John Cabot

39. What year was Nunavut created?
a) 1867
b) 1949
c) 1982
d) 1999

40. Which level of government is responsible for education and health care?
a) Federal
b) Provincial/Territorial
c) Shared
d) Municipal

41. Which level of government is responsible for garbage collection and firefighting?
a) Federal
b) Provincial
c) Municipal
d) Shared

42. Which day commemorates Canada's victory at Vimy Ridge in 1917?
a) November 11
b) April 9
c) July 1

d) May 25

43. Who was the first woman elected as a Member of Parliament in Canada?
a) Emily Murphy
b) Agnes Macphail
c) Nellie McClung
d) Emily Stowe

44. What is the significance of the Underground Railroad in Canadian history?
a) It was Canada's first railway
b) It brought thousands of enslaved people from the U.S. to freedom in Canada
c) It was built during Confederation
d) It connected provinces by trade

45. What is the role of the RCMP?
a) To run elections
b) To represent the Sovereign
c) To keep Canadians safe and enforce federal law
d) To manage the Senate

46. What is the national anthem of Canada?
a) God Save the King
b) The Maple Leaf Forever
c) O Canada
d) From Sea to Sea

47. What year was *O Canada* proclaimed as the national anthem?
a) 1867
b) 1921
c) 1965
d) 1980

48. Which Canadian is known for the Marathon of Hope?

a) Rick Hansen

b) Donovan Bailey

c) Terry Fox

d) Wayne Gretzky

49. Which Canadian circled the globe in a wheelchair to raise funds for spinal cord research?

a) Terry Fox

b) Rick Hansen

c) Donovan Bailey

d) Mike Lazaridis

50. What is the Oath of Citizenship?

a) A promise to obey provincial laws

b) A pledge of loyalty to the Sovereign and to Canada, obeying its laws and fulfilling citizen duties

c) A promise to pay taxes on time

d) A pledge to vote in every election

* * *

Answer Key

1. a
2. b
3. b
4. a
5. b
6. b
7. c
8. a

9. b
10. c
11. a
12. c
13. b
14. b
15. b
16. c
17. b
18. b
19. b
20. c
21. b
22. b
23. b
24. b
25. a
26. b
27. b
28. c
29. c
30. a
31. d
32. b
33. a
34. b
35. c
36. a
37. c
38. b
39. d
40. b
41. c

42. b
43. b
44. b
45. c
46. c
47. d
48. c
49. b
50. b

Made in the USA
Monee, IL
04 November 2026

67377476R00036